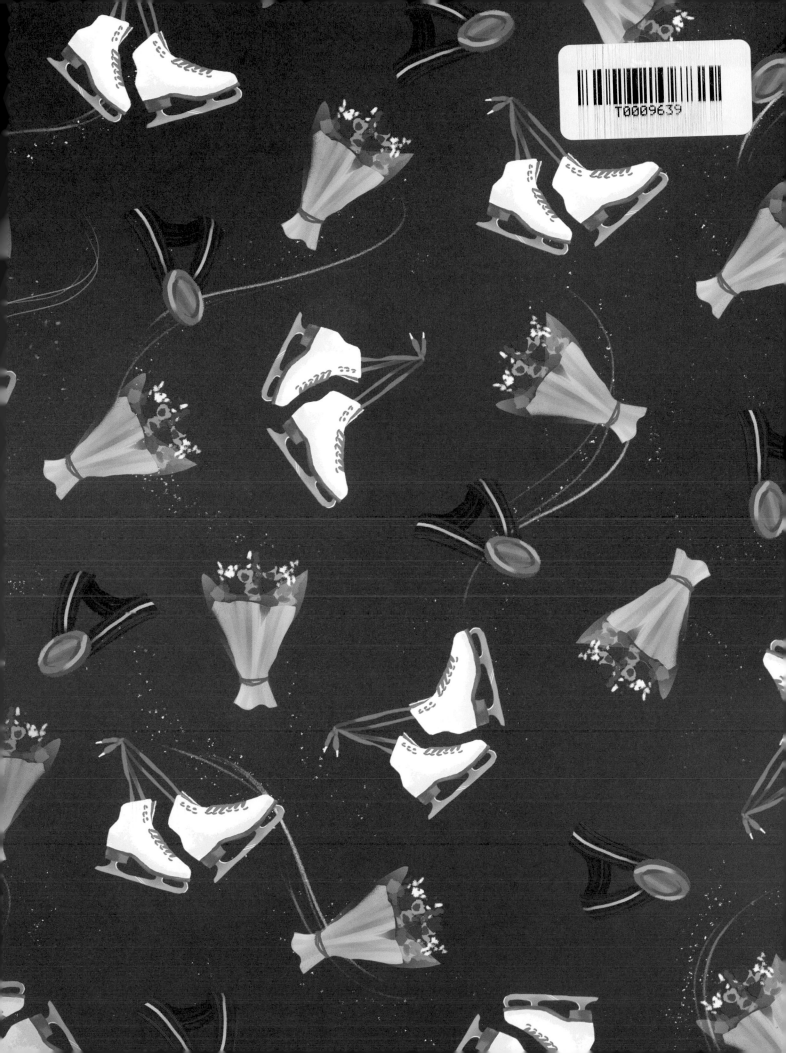

AN ILLUSTRATED BIOGRAPY OF SURYA BONALY

FEARLESS HEART

THE LEGACY OF AN OLYMPIC FIGURE SKATER

By **Frank Murphy**
with **Surya Bonaly**

Art by **Anastasia
Magloire Williams**

No part of this publication may be reproduced, stored in a retrieval system, or transmitted in any form by any means,
electronic, mechanical, photocopying, or otherwise, without the prior written permission of the publisher,
Triumph Books LLC, 814 North Franklin Street, Chicago, Illinois 60610.
Library of Congress Cataloging in Publication Data available upon request.
Printed in U.S.A. ISBN: 978-1-62937-934-0

Her Dawn.

December 15th, 1973.
A beautiful
baby girl
named Claudine
is born
in Nice, France.

Adopted eighteen months later
by a man and woman
Suzanne and Gorges Bonaly.

And Claudine became...

their sun,

their star,

their **Surya**.

Her Dream.

By 10 years old...
Surya knew
she wanted to spend her life on the ice.
Everyday.
All day.

She knew she could
be like her coach,
a national champion.

She loved the joy of
her skates scratching
the ice,

the freedom of

F   L   Y   I   N   G

in the air

and

FLOATING

above
the
frozen
white
ice

She practiced all that she saw.

One skate helped her

higher.

P
M
U
J

The other helped her glide
gracefully.
Double axels.
Triple toe loops.
And spins.
Again and again.

And again.

She didn't always finish first,
So she worked harder.
And harder.

And soon,
Surya's young career became filled with

1ST PLACE

Her Rise.

European champion 5 straight times.
And 13 more times – She was ranked number 1.
Surya was named French champion
9 straight times.

Around the globe,
the hearts of children
leaped with ice skating dreams.
And they imagined themselves

spinning

and looping

like fire

like the sun

in radiant gold

like **Surya**.

Striking a pose...
then taking off...
...with tremendous speed, hurling into jumps.

Soaring through the air.
With power and pride and precision.

Jump after jump after jump.
Wanting to be the combo queen of the ice
Wishing and working
...stepping, gliding, running into original jumps,

Hand springs and even...
back flips!

In brilliant and bedazzled costumes.
Electric colored eye shadow.
Passion in her heart.

Surya was determined to be...
the first Surya! The only Surya!
There ever will be.
There ever was.

Her Judges.

They said
there are rules in figure skating.
Ways a skater is supposed to be.

To move.

To speak.

To look.

They said
she should look like everyone else.

Skate like everyone else.
She would score high if she followed their rules.

But Surya didn't follow. And her innovation was not allowed.

The judges couldn't deny Surya her technical merit.
But they never rewarded *her* artistry.

They said—
"She has to work on her grace."
"She needs to stop jumping and learn to skate..."
"There's raw talent, but she's not refined."

But her fans knew
what her critics wouldn't
say out loud.

The judges didn't want a
Black figure skater,
skating the way she wanted.
And, maybe,
they didn't want a
Black figure skater
at all.

The judges said—
"She's too muscular."
"She isn't elegant enough."
They said
her skates didn't sound right
as they carved the ice.

So Surya made a choice.

Her Strength.

After years of hearing
her critics,
the noise...
"Not graceful enough."
"You skate in straight lines, you need to create
circles."
And worst of all

 "Second place.........."

 "Second place.........."

Surya's heart grew stronger.
She refused to quit.
She fought back
the only way she knew she could.

She practiced.
Practiced
and practiced
and practiced,
more.

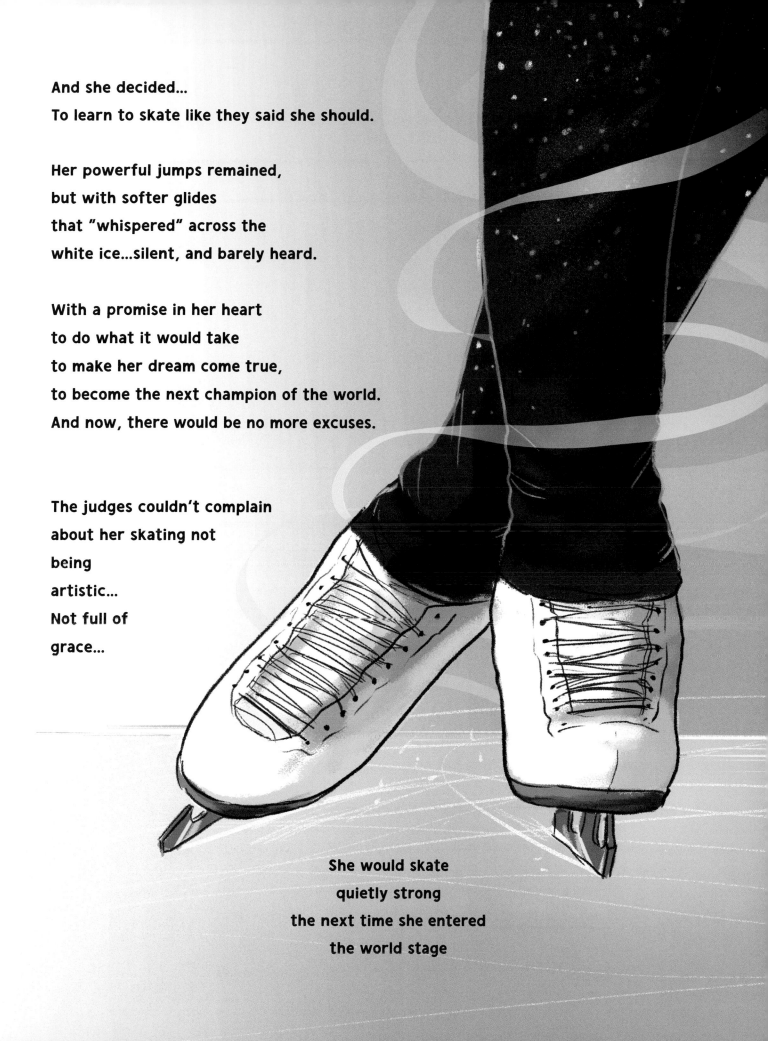

And she decided...
To learn to skate like they said she should.

Her powerful jumps remained,
but with softer glides
that "whispered" across the
white ice...silent, and barely heard.

With a promise in her heart
to do what it would take
to make her dream come true,
to become the next champion of the world.
And now, there would be no more excuses.

The judges couldn't complain
about her skating not
being
artistic...
Not full of
grace...

She would skate
quietly strong
the next time she entered
the world stage

Her Moment.

1994. Japan.
World Championships.

With her...
Hopeful. Heart.
More than ready this time.
To become
the
number
one
figure skater in the world.

She started with a double axel.
Then triple, triple, triple.
Her skates did whisper across the ice
and
her body floated with grace.
Her spins tight.
Her spins fast.
And her turns rounded circles.
Surya skated the most magnificent routine
of her life.
Four and a half minutes of pure grace
and great power on the ice!
The scores...

Tie...
...between Surya and the skater from Japan.
The judges would
vote
to decide
"second place".

The judges voted – 4 to 5 in favor of Surya...
...being "second place."
She did not win.
AGAIN.

The announcer called out
 the winner's name first.
She skated out
to the cheers of her home country.

The announcer called out Surya's name,
second.
...and the crowd waited.
The world waited...
"...and reluctantly she arrives."
Surya skated onto the white ice,
her heart frozen.

She raised her arms to the cheering
crowd.
She skated to the first place skater.
Surya honored her,
kissing each cheek.
And smiling.
She skated to the podium meant for
"second place".
And then...

Surya arrived,
but refused to
stand
on that second place podium.

2

The official presented the "first place"
skater with the

GOLD MEDAL.

The official looked toward Surya.

He hesitated.

And hesitated.

He motioned to Surya
to step upon the podium.

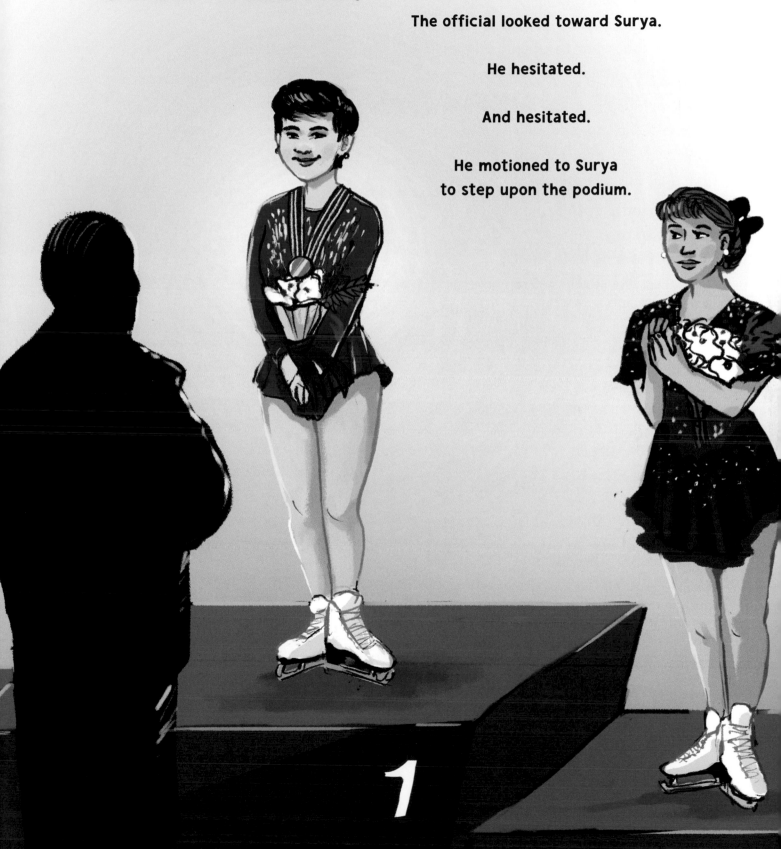

Surya resisted.

She stood her place.
He stepped toward her.
He placed the silver medal around her
neck. He shook her hand and then...
...pulled her, forcing her up, up
onto the podium.
Surya stood.

She knew she did not belong
on a "second place" podium.
Not on this day.
And With. Her. Broken. Heart.
She pulled the silver medal
off
her neck.

The crowd gasped.

But freedom raised Surya's chin a little higher!
She held the medal and ribbon at her side.
Tangled
in her hand
like her emotions

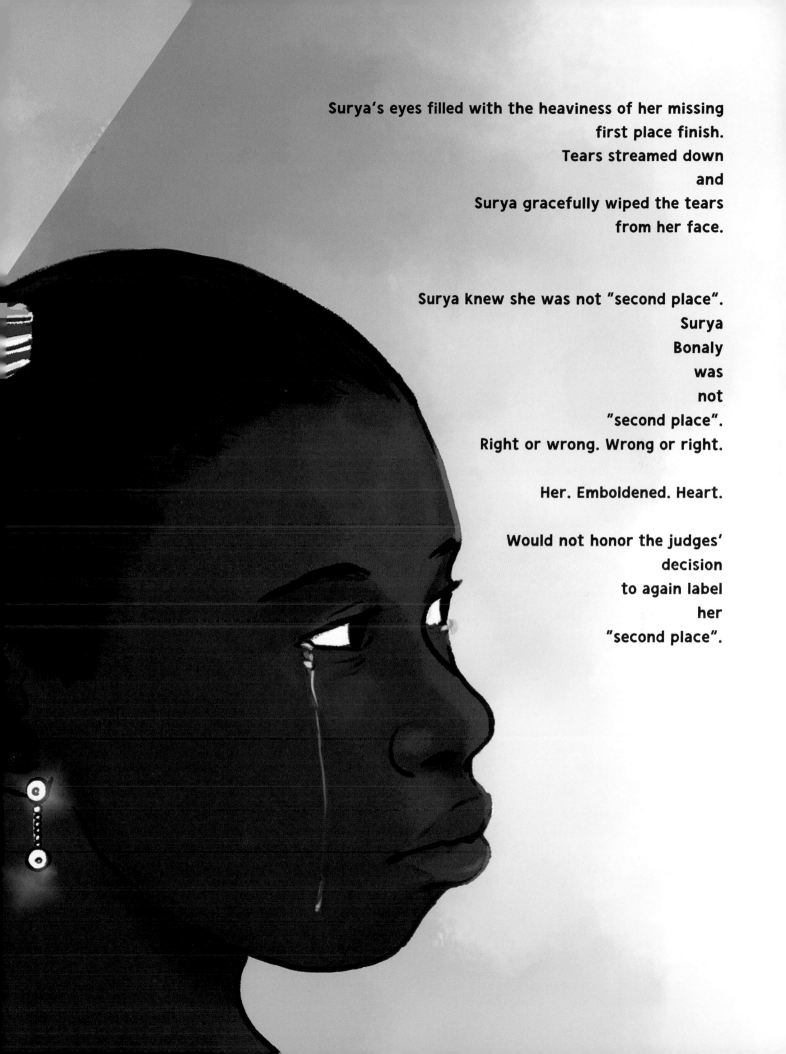

Surya's eyes filled with the heaviness of her missing
first place finish.
Tears streamed down
and
Surya gracefully wiped the tears
from her face.

Surya knew she was not "second place".
Surya
Bonaly
was
not
"second place".
Right or wrong. Wrong or right.

Her. Emboldened. Heart.

Would not honor the judges'
decision
to again label
her
"second place".

The crowd of reporters were waiting.
Their words echoing and ringing in
Surya's ears.

" Surya..?"

" Surya why?"

"Why?"

" What happened
Surya?"

" Are they **unfair**
to you, Surya?"

" Surya **why** did you **not**
accept the medal?"

" What was the **problem**?"

Surya's answers were not in her words.
They could only be found in her tears
at the moment each one finally

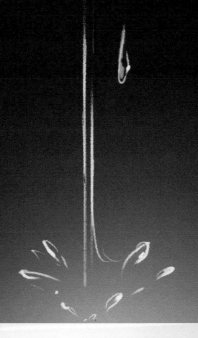

landed
on the frozen-white ice.

And became nothing.
Where no one was
looking.

1995. England.
World Championships again.

Determined. Again.
Hopeful. Again.
But...
"second place"
...again.

Her Fearless Heart.

1998. Nagano, Japan.
The Olympics.

Surya's Achilles—injured.
Her heart—fearless, again.
Surya wanted to skate among the best
one last time.
Surya struck a pose.
And then she took

off...

"Triple toe...

Triple Sal..."

Half loop...

...and Surya stumbled and
fell.
Surya got up—full of grace...
...she kept skating.
Persisting with...
Speed.
Beauty.
And heart.
Fearless.
She determined herself
to show
that she could land that triple
Salchow.

Surya raced into it...Spinning and soaring into...

"Triple Salchow.....proving to everyone
that she can land it!"

And Surya fought through the pain...
And her skating continued.
Determined.

Deep inside, her heart spoke to her,

"I need to do this."

She spun to her left, skating backward.
Clenched her fists...
Lifted her arms to the sky....

Surya leaned forward, bending her left
leg...threw her arms behind her...
And...

...catapulted her body **upside down,**

into the air.

Almost magically.

NAGANO 1998

her legs backward and forward.
Into a split position.

She spun around and landed
on just one skate.

Surya continued skating backward
on just one skate!

Smiling.
Surya's smile shined.
And the crowd gasped
and then erupted, cheering loudly.
And they kept cheering

and cheering...

NAGANO 1998

Surya finished skating.
Pleasing her fans first, she faced
the roaring crowd,

...she had stayed true to herself.

with her back to the judges.
Surya knew...
by accomplishing this historic backflip,
landing
on just *one* skate...

To her heart,
her fearless heart.

Her trademark!

A move no one had ever
accomplished, not then,
not since...
Her first place finish.

Unstoppable.
Unrepeatable.

And Surya whispered in her soul,
as she turned to face the judges.

They will never forget me now.

Surya Bonaly

Photo credit: LYDIE/ NIVIERE/NIKO/SIPA/ Newscom

After her historic backflip on one skate at the Olympics in 1998, Surya Bonaly retired from competitive amateur skating and went on to have an active professional career skating with freedom, athleticism, and grace in various ice shows and events. Finally, without the intense judging and regulation of competitive skating, Surya could perform flips and combinations to her heart's content, and to the contentment of her enraptured audience.

Today, Surya works as a skating coach in Minnesota. She passes on her passionate love of skating and her fearless spirit to her students, who continue to inspire her in turn. Alongside coaching, Surya is an active philanthropist, activist, and public speaker.

Photo credit: Keystone/Laurent Gillieron/AP Images

DID YOU KNOW?

FUN FACTS ABOUT SURYA

- **Many of Surya's colorful, iconic outfits were made by her mother, Suzanne**

- **Surya excelled in gymnastics before choosing to focus on figure skating, her true passion**

- **The name Surya is Sanskrit for "Sun"**

- **Surya is the first and only skater to land a backflip on one skate!**

- **Surya is known as the "combination queen"—she was the first female skater to attempt many combinations most deemed too difficult or risky**

Photo credit: Glen Stubbe/ ZUMA Press/Newscom

Photo credit: BENAROCH/ SIPA/Newscom

Krista Hicks Benson/Icon SMI 751/Krista Hicks Benson/Icon SMI/Newscom

ABOUT THE AUTHOR

Frank Murphy has been teaching elementary school for over 30 years and writing children's books for over 20 years. The author of many award-winning picture books and beginning readers, this is his first book with Triumph Books. He lives near Philadelphia with his family and he is a terrible ice skater!

AUTHOR'S NOTE: *The NPR program RadioLab was my doorway into the beginning of telling Surya's story. In 2018, I listened to her story being told on my local station, WHYY in Philly. Listening, I remembered seeing Surya on TV in the '90s. Hearing Surya's story captivated me and inspired me to write a short poem about her. Then, I was compelled to contact Surya to interview her because I knew I could grow that poem into a picture book. In April 2019, myself and my class interviewed Surya over the phone, learning about her experiences. A month later, Surya invited me to Harlem to watch the filming of a Netflix documentary about her career. It took four years of collaboration: crafting and forming the text with Surya, marrying the text with Ana's stunning art, and constructing the book with the team at Triumph. It is an honor to finally be able to bring this book to life and to have done it with Surya's guidance and blessing. I chose to craft the text in free verse poetry to reflect the style of Surya's skating—because Surya truly was poetry on ice.*

ABOUT THE ILLUSTRATOR

Anastasia Magloire Williams is an illustrator and visual storyteller working in children's literature and entertainment media. Her artistic mission is to elevate untold stories with bright colors, evocative lines, and painterly application of digital art mediums. When she is not bringing characters and concepts to life for her clients, she enjoys reading fantasy novels and gaming with her husband, Ryan. Illustrating this book inspired her to learn how to ice skate—wish her luck! You can see more of her work at **www.anadraws.com**

ABOUT THE PUBLISHER

Triumph Books is the nation's leading sports book publisher—an independent publisher founded in 1989. In addition to working with some of the most celebrated coaches and athletes in the world, they publish oral and team histories, pictorials, and rule books for every major American sports league. Triumph Books seeks to champion authors and stories that reflect the beautifully diverse and colorful world we share, uplifting readers with stories of perseverance, courage, and incredible strength.

TRIUMPH
B O O K S

TRIUMPHBOOKS**.COM**
🔲🐦📷 @TRIUMPHBOOKS